KID

MILLIONAIRE

13-Digit ISBN: 9781604336535
10-Digit ISBN: 1604336536

This book may be ordered by mail from the publisher. Please include $5.99 for postage and handling. Please support your local bookseller first!

Books published by Cider Mill Press Book Publishers are available at special discounts for bulk purchases in the United States by corporations, institutions, and other organizations. For more information, please contact the publisher.

Applesauce Press is an imprint of
Cider Mill Press Book Publishers
"Where good books are ready for press"
PO Box 454
12 Spring Street
Kennebunkport, Maine 04046

Visit us on the Web! www.cidermillpress.com

Design by Melissa Gerber
Illustrations by Annalisa Sheldahl
Typography: A year without rain, Andes, Adobe Garamond Pro, Amatic Bold, Archive Antique Extended, Brandon Printed One, Canvas Icons, Eveleth, Fanwood, Festiva Letters, Growler Script, Nexa Rust, Pinto No_1, and Pringleton

Printed in the United States
1 2 3 4 5 6 7 8 9 0
First Edition

KID
MILLIONAIRE

By Matthew Eliot

Kennebunkport, Maine

TABLE *of* CONTENTS

STARTING UP:
Earning and Saving

WHAT YOU'LL LEARN:

- The Importance of Saving
- How to Look for Work Opportunities
- Tracking Your Earnings and Savings
- Setting Goals and Sticking to Them
- How to Divide Your Money Between Spendings and Savings
- How to Use Apps to Increase Your Financial Skills

BUSINESS IDEAS COVERED:

- ✓ Part-time job
- ✓ Volunteer
- ✓ Crafting and building
- ✓ Cleaning and recycling
- ✓ Holiday help

In order to save up for something you want, you need to have enough money to save. As a kid, this can be somewhat tricky. Even if you're lucky enough to receive a weekly allowance, it's probably too small to think about putting a portion of it away. Now, if you can supplement that allowance with other work, you've got some options!

As you will see, the world is full of opportunities to make money. Especially for kids! You have the creativity, energy, and freedom to try things most people wouldn't dare. Put these advantages to work and watch your fortunes change. The easiest way to earn money is to do something for someone else. This is called providing a service. Most people earn a living this way: the waiters at your favorite restaurant, your teachers at school, and even your family doctor! They each have specific skills that people are willing to pay them for.

Your first job is to figure out what services the people around you need. Maybe you notice that the leaves are piling up in your neighbor's yard. Or maybe you overhear one of your parents' friends complaining about shoveling their driveway this winter. Or you may notice a "Help Wanted" sign in the window at a nearby store or café. These are all cries for help! Pleas for your services!

And, after reading this book, you'll have no trouble hearing them and cashing in.

THE PART-TIME JOB

Many a young investor began their career with a part-time job during the summer or after school. But be advised: Every state has different rules about work permits, so ask your parents or future supervisor about the specific guidelines in your area.

HOW TO GET STARTED:

Check your local craigslist.org site for job listings. The site divides the available jobs into a number of categories, so there's a good chance you'll find something that fits. But don't just limit your search to the computer. Next time you're walking around with a friend or one of your parents, keep an eye out for signs asking for assistance in store and restaurant windows. And if your family gets the local newspaper, or if you find yourself at the library, browse the classified ads.

Most importantly, get out there and talk to people! Word of mouth is tremendously powerful when you're looking for a job. Ask your friends' parents and your parents' friends if they know of anyone who may be hiring or if they need a helping hand. If there's a specific place you'd like to work, don't just fill out an application or send in a resume. Head on over and talk to a supervisor or manager. If they've met you, your application may receive greater consideration than those who are just a name on a piece of paper. You've put in the extra effort and that makes a difference. Call the circulation departments of your local newspapers. Would they hire you to deliver papers each morning in your own neighborhood or one close by?

Summer is a great time to find part-time work; stores are usually looking for additional hands to help out. You can try your local ice cream stand, sandwich shop, or the stores in the mall. A part-time job can be fun and rewarding, but if you work during the school year, make sure your homework and school-related extra curricular activities come first. Don't be afraid to ask your boss for fewer hours if your grades begin to suffer.

THE VOLUNTEER

By definition, a volunteer does work for free. So why would someone interested in putting a big pile of money together bother with a gig that doesn't pay anything? Here's a little secret: Through volunteer work, you can gain valuable experience that will help you get a better paying, more interesting job later on. Intrigued? Read on . . .

HOW TO GET STARTED:

Suppose you are interested in being a journalist or a doctor, but you haven't gone to college. There's nothing a newspaper or a hospital can hire you to do, right? Not so fast. There are probably many opportunities at either of those places, and they may be more than happy for your help, so long as they don't have to pay you for it.

For example, hospitals often have a whole team of young volunteers (sometimes called "candy stripers") to help with many different things: paperwork, delivering food or flowers, and visiting with patients. On occasion, local newspapers bring on volunteers to make phone calls, take pictures, update their web site, or even help out around the newsroom.

Volunteer opportunities may also be available at your local animal shelter, library, museum, or television station. If one of these careers sounds exciting, drop this book right now and look into it! You won't be getting paid but you will receive plenty of valuable on-the-job training. This preparation not only puts you ahead of most of the kids your age, it also makes you more attractive to the people you've helped out. Now that they know you a bit better, they'll be more likely to hire you when a position becomes available.

SETTING GOALS & SAVING UP

Once you have money coming in, also known as an income, you can afford to buy more than just junk food. Maybe that purchase is a video game or some cool clothes you've had your eye on.

But hold on just a second! If you want to turn your small pile of dough into an item of real value: a mountain bike, an electric guitar, a car, or one million dollars, you can't spend your salary the second you earn it. You have to save some!

Saving up your hard-earned money can be difficult. It's natural to want to enjoy the profit that comes out of those labors. But if you can stay strong, stick to a budget, and store some money away, you'll reap the benefits for the rest of your life. You will also find them far more enjoyable than the temporary satisfaction junk food or a new video game provides.

One method that can really help you save is setting a goal. Once a goal has been set, you can figure out the best path to get you there. Are you looking to purchase a musical instrument or a laptop, where you can simply put your money in a drawer until you have enough? Or is it an item that will take some time and allow you to take advantage of an interest-bearing bank account? Or are you looking to invest in something so long-term (a car, college) that a CD or a bond would be your best option?

Setting a goal not only teaches you how to save and invest, it will also illustrate the value of planning and thinking about what you want in the long run. Once you have the end result in mind, it becomes easier

11

and easier to keep yourself from blowing all your earnings.

That doesn't mean you have to save every penny you bring in. Here's an idea: for every three dollars you earn, save one of those dollars for long-term investments, one for short-term savings, and one for spending money. Place each dollar into a different envelope or jar. Remember not to raid your bank when you run out of spending money! Plan ahead so that doesn't happen. Trust me, it'll be worth it.

TRACKING YOUR ALLOWANCE AND EARNINGS

Saving is a good way to monitor your spending, but it's also smart to keep tabs on how much money you've got coming in. If you always know where you stand, you'll be able to act accordingly. If you're just guessing, you may find yourself dipping into your savings the next time you want to go see the latest superhero movie with friends.

You're going to want to track your income and you don't want to have to count out your money each payday to total your current earnings.

One smart option is starting a spreadsheet with a column for each job and another for the amount earned. Then you can create an additional spreadsheet that tracks your expenses.

A spreadsheet is nice because it can do a lot of the math for you and many future employers will be happy that you're familiar with the program. (And it doesn't have to be fancy!)

The main objective is keeping track of your money, which includes how much you are earning from each job and what you're spending it on. You can do this with nothing more than a notebook and a calculator. Just

make sure you remain organized! Do this, and you'll always know what to do when you see something you want to buy or when someone asks you to do something fun.

This is also a helpful strategy when you obtain a bank account. The bank will supply you with a little book where you can keep track of your deposits and withdrawals. Make a habit of writing each one down and then add or subtract that amount from the total in there beforehand. The bank will provide you with a statement each month, but it's a good idea to keep track of it on your own. Everyone makes mistakes, even banks! If you're paying close attention, these mistakes won't cost you a thing.

Another great online tool for tracking your finances is Mint.com. This website connects to your bank account and will break down your spending and savings into categories (such as shopping, recreation, food, etc.). The breakdowns allow you to see where you can cut back if you're looking to save more and provide valuable information if you're wondering where all your hard-earned money has gone.

APPS FOR DEVELOPING SAVING SKILLS AND STRATEGIES

➡ **Bee Farming** by Five Deer Ltd., $1.99

While you're having a blast selling honey and purchasing bees, this app is also teaching you how to run a business, how to strategize, and how to use creativity to help your business grow.

➡ **Savings Spree** by Money Savvy Generation, $5.99

An enjoyable game show app where you assess your financial knowledge and acquire helpful skills like goal making, spending, donating and investing! The app also illustrates how expensive surprises and accidents can be, pointing out that it's always a good idea to have a little bit of a monetary cushion room.

➡ **Green$treets: Unleash the Loot!** by GreenStreet Commons, Inc., Free

A perfect game for animal lovers! This fun app allows the user to work within a budget to save their favorite endangered animals. They will learn important financial and math skills and start to understand how big of a difference money and charity can make.

➡ **P2K Money** by Loconuts, Inc., Free

This app makes it easy to gauge how close you are to that new game, bike or guitar. Use it to keep tabs on your income and expenses and you'll always know where you stand.

➡ **Bankaroo by BrightAct LLC.,** Free

An 11-year-old girl designed this app, so she knows exactly where you're coming from! This app functions just like a financial advisor where you enter your income and allowance, set your target and put funds toward it.

➡ **Allowance+ Bank of Mom and Dad by** Kincentrix Inc., Free

This app aids parents in tracking your allowance. You then work together to help build financial understanding. It's a great way to show them you're responsible and ready for a little more independence.

Here are a few more ideas:

- Make Birdhouses – Take a look in your neighbors' yards—there's a good chance you'll see a bird feeder or a birdhouse there. If you're handy with woodworking tools, there's a great opportunity to spruce up someone's outside decor, increase their enjoyment, and hone your skills—all while making some great money!

- Recycling – If your town has a recycling program, that's great! If they don't, that's great for you! With a little bit of organization and hustle, you can get your own program going. Gather up people's cans, metals and bottles, and transport them to the nearest recycling facility. You'll make some money while helping the environment—what a great deal!

- Cleaning Homes – As busy as people are nowadays, it's hard to keep things neat and orderly. And if you're willing to get your hands dirty, this is a great way to make a few extra bucks on the weekend. Tell Mom and Dad that you're willing to give the house a deep clean every Saturday and watch their eyes light up! Or offer your services around the neighborhood—you're sure to clean up!

- Baking Cookies and Making Candy for the Holidays – As you may have noticed, people like to indulge themselves around the holidays. You can capitalize on this tendency by perfecting a couple of treats. Do this, and you'll become part of people's holiday traditions—and make enough money that you'll be able to take it easy the rest of the year!

- Giftwrapping – People are usually so busy around the holidays that they barely have the time to shop for all their gifts—never mind get them wrapped. Right after Thanksgiving, put up some signs around town that announce you're available to help out with giftwrapping. Chances are you'll have a line of relieved individuals at your door!

- Design Greeting Cards & Invitations – Are you a wizard at designing stuff on the computer? Put that expertise to use and provide people with memorable greeting cards and invitations for the most important days and people in their lives! All you need is a computer and some high-quality paper to print them on. And if you're skeptical about the amount of money you can make doing this, check out Cameron Johnson in the Kid Millionaire Stories chapter.

SMALL, INDEPENDENT BUSINESS

WHAT YOU'LL LEARN:

- The Basics of Starting a Business
- How to Gather Ideas for Your Endeavor
- Assessing the Value of Your Time
- Ways to Expand on a few Tried and True Kid Businesses
- How to be a Professional
- The Importance of Communicating with Clients

BUSINESS IDEAS COVERED:

- ✓ Lawnmowing/Landscaping
- ✓ Lemonade Stand
- ✓ Tutoring
- ✓ Golf caddy
- ✓ Bike messenger
- ✓ Dog-walking/Pet sitting
- ✓ Magician

You've mastered your chores, stayed on top of your schoolwork, and even helped the elderly neighbor down the street. But maybe you're looking for something bigger, a job that allows you to take charge. If so, make the leap and start your own business!

An entrepreneur is someone who invests their time and money into a new business. This can be risky since many new businesses fail within the first year. But it can also be extremely fun and very rewarding, not to mention a tremendous learning experience. If you're intrigued by the idea of striking out on your own here are a few you should know:

- Some business ideas may work out better than others depending on where you live and what people will (or will not) pay for. Starting your own business is another instance where talking to people will really help. Ask around and see what services people feel are missing in your neighborhood. Once you hear of something that seems doable, you can be up and running. Give a lot of thought to how much your time is worth. Consider the lowest amount you'd be happy earning for each hour you spend working and price your work accordingly. You definitely want to have this squared away before you tell someone how much you charge. This can be difficult to estimate when you're first starting out, but don't worry. After a few jobs where you feel like you're giving far more than you're receiving, you'll adjust your price accordingly.

- Keep track of how much money you spend on supplies and materials each week. Add it up. Are you making a profit or actually losing money? Always be on the lookout for ways you can cut costs and increase your profits.

Eager to get your own business going but don't know exactly what you'd like to do? Read on! We've got a few tried-and-true businesses that have been sustaining readers your age since the dawn of time.

THE CLASSIC ENTREPRENEURIAL JOBS

LAWN MOWING

What you'll need:

➡ A lawnmower

➡ Special yard waste bags for certain areas

HOW TO GET STARTED:

Mowing your neighbors' lawns is a great way to start your business. Once you have a group of devoted customers and an idea of how much materials (gas, tools, trash/yard waste bags) are going to cost, think about expanding both your territory and what services you offer. Weeding, raking, and spreading bark mulch (fertilizer for a garden) are all great additions to offer in your expansion. With a little bit of luck, you'll soon find yourself in charge of a full-service lawn care business!

Think about what services you can offer to set your business apart from all the other lawn care entrepreneurs in

the area. Perhaps your town prefers organic gardening. If so, you can turn your lawn clippings into quality compost that people will pay top dollar for. Composting is also a great way to reduce the waste in your own household and help the environment, so everybody wins! For more information on composting visit: http://www.planetnatural.com/composting-101.

Just because the ground is covered with snow doesn't mean your business needs to take a hit. You've already found a group of people who trust you and value your work. So buy a shovel or two, an ice scraper, and a bag of salt, and turn your lawn care business into one that also does snow and ice removal. You'll keep your clients happy and your pockets full throughout the year!

LEMONADE STAND

By taking this classic business away from your front yard, you can really cash in.

What you'll need:

➡ A portable cooler

➡ A few reusable ice packs

➡ Several dozen bottles of water, soda, or juice

➡ A hip-pack for holding money and making change

HOW TO GET STARTED:

Depending on where you want to sell your product you may need a permit from your local town hall. Make sure to get your paperwork squared away before diving in. Buy your ingredients and supplies in bulk at a discount or wholesale store to maximize profit. Make sure to compare prices at different stores. Also, pay attention to the flyers from your local grocery stores which advertise items on sale. You just may get lucky and be able to stock up on the cheap!

Share your plans with your parents. Chances are, you'll need their help carting your beverages around town.

Once you've made a few batches, load up a cooler and hit the beach! Try to set up shop where lots of people pass by, like the parking lot, or even the bathrooms. If there's a park or soccer field near your house, these can also be good options.

If you'd like to get some exercise while working, try walking along the beach and bringing the refreshment right to your customers. People love to be waited on and are often willing to pay more for something if it is convenient. Don't be afraid to test out higher prices for your walk-up service.

TUTOR CLASSMATES

Are you a math whiz, history buff, or love science? Put your knowledge to use and help others understand what comes so naturally to you.

What you'll need:

➡ School supplies:

➡ Paper, pencils, a calculator, etc.

HOW TO GET STARTED:

Does your client need help with every subject? Are they looking for a weekly review session or do they only want help right before a big test? Start off by assessing their understanding of the subject and create a plan on how often you'll be meeting and for how long.

Find a clean, quiet space, preferably one that has a good-sized table and no distractions! Libraries are perfect for this and often have meeting rooms that you can reserve. A large coffee shop where you can find a spot away from any noise is another good option.

Make sure you're always well prepared! Take some time to review the material you'll be discussing before your study session, especially if it's been a while since you last did long division or wrote a report on The Revolutionary War.

Remember this: Patience and your ability to communicate are the most important traits you'll need if you want to be a successful tutor. Your knowledge is impressive, but if you can't listen to your clients or simplify things that come so easily to you, their struggles are going to continue.

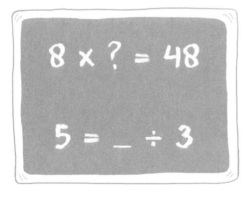

GO WITH WHAT YOU'RE GOOD AT!

Not drawn to any of the above options? Don't worry! Being passionate about what you do is one of the most important things to focus on when starting your own business. It will help you keep going when times get tough.

So what are you passionate about? What are you good at? How do you enjoy spending your time? Whatever it is, there's a good chance that, with a little bit of creative thinking, you can make an occupation out of it.

Here are a few more ideas:

- If you like to golf, think about offering your services at a nearby club as a caddy. You'll learn a lot about the game and meet a lot of interesting people.

- If you like to ride your bike, see if you can locate a bike messenger/delivery service needed in your town. People are always pressed for time—if you're willing to do some of the running around for them, they'll be happy to compensate you for it.

- Are you an animal lover? Consider starting a dog walking/pet care business. Pet owners will pay top dollar to find people they can trust with their animals.

- Are you someone who loves

magic and card tricks? Practice your tricks at home until you've perfected them and then hire yourself out for people's parties! You'll provide people with endless joy and wonder and keep your pockets full while pursuing one of your passions—pretty magical.

The point of being an entrepreneur is to try and make money doing something you love. So take whatever hobbies or interests you're really dedicated to and give it a go!

BEING AN ENTREPRENEUR MEANS BEING A PRO

All the passion in the world won't mean a thing if people can't trust you. So always remember to be professional. Do what you say you will do when you say you will do it. If something is taking longer than you thought, or if an emergency comes up, make sure you speak with the people who are relying on your services. Individuals like to work with folks they can count on. Once word gets out that you're reliable, you'll have no trouble earning money. Another aspect of being a business owner is looking the part. So dress nicely. Appearance is important when you're working for others, whether you like it or not. People may find it harder to trust someone who looks sloppy, so don't give them any reason to doubt you. Wear clean, unwrinkled clothes, and make sure your hair is combed!

WORLD WIDE WEB OF OPPORTUNITY

WHAT YOU'LL LEARN:

- Taking Advantage of the Numerous Opportunities Online
- How to Distinguish Yourself from the Crowd
- The Importance of Building an Audience/Network
- Using the Internet to Market Your Business
- The Need to Establish a Reliable Reputation

BUSINESS IDEAS COVERED:

- ✓ Building websites & squarespace sites
- ✓ Building apps
- ✓ Blogging
- ✓ Computer help
- ✓ Managing social media

We feel the incredible impact of technology every day. It's made so many things easier and has provided access to opportunities, which once seemed possible only in dreams.

For you, this is an amazing piece of luck. Not only have a lot of the restrictions that would have kept you away from such lucrative territory vanished, but the ease in which your generation uses computers, tablets and smartphones actually puts you at an advantage over many of your elders.

BUILDING WEBSITES AND APPS

As you can probably guess, the Internet has put plenty of money up for grabs. Read on to see how you can get your share.

CREATE A WEBSITE

What you'll need:

➡ A computer

➡ Some knowledge of programming and web design to decide what platform to use and your domain name

➡ Web publishing software to launch your site

You probably spend a portion of each day scrolling through your favorite sites to see if there's anything new going on. Well, millions of people do the exact same thing. If you can create a site that makes its way into your target audience's daily routine, you'll be on easy street in no time. As the Internet is a vast space with endless options, it can be difficult to know what direction you want to go in. Here are a few ideas that can help you get started.

BUILD A FANSITE

You may already have a go to website that features a subject or hobby you love but always remember the first rule of making money: Provide someone with something else they want! Use the expertise you employed to build your own website that focuses on a sub-category or a completely different category that you know to be hugely popular. It could be a band, a television show, or a particular comic book character. Animals and  sports teams also have the ability to draw a massive following. Build a website on one of these topics and include a section that is devoted to a fan club. Ask the people interested in joining this community of like-minded fanatics for a small membership fee ($10-$20 per person) and, if people think it's worth it Voila! You're on your way to start making some revenue !

Your website's success will likely depend on two things: how catchy the site's name is and how cool it looks. People want sites that are easy to remember, so give your domain name plenty of thought before you launch. Web surfers also want to spend their time on a site that looks nice and runs smoothly, so keep this in mind during the construction phase.

BUILD SITES FOR OTHERS

You're not the only one who has noticed the financial potential that exists on the Web. All kinds of business owners and artists view the Internet as the key to making their dreams a reality. But many of these folks may not have your ability and level of comfort with technology. By offering to build them a website, you can fill your pockets!

When you're first starting out, offer to design a few websites for free (or for very cheap). Later, when you're ready to start charging for what your time is really worth, you'll have a few examples for potential clients to look at.

A good way to grab clients is to take a look at the current websites for restaurants and other businesses in your town. Some may not have a site and want one, while others may have one that is severely out of date, but no time to update it themselves. Contact their owners and offer your services. After you have finished a site for someone, you can drum up a bit of extra money by offering to stay on as the site's Webmaster: fixing crashes and redesigning certain areas of the site when needed.

Once you really know your stuff, contact the owners of websites that could use a redesign and offer to help them out. So long as you're respectful and positive, since they may have designed the site themselves, it can't hurt to ask.

A SECRET ABOUT SQUARESPACE

Squarespace is a platform that provides ready-made website templates and the bandwidth to host a site. While this may seem like a threat to your promising web design career, Squarespace still requires quite a bit of know-how if you want a website that looks both slick and impressive meaning there will still be considerable opportunity for you to use  your skills to help out discouraged potential clients. It's a good idea to get comfortable with Squarespace and learn all the tricks needed to maximize the potential of one of their sites. Once you do, you'll be able to serve those who are drawn to this platform, and expend far less time and energy than you would building a site from scratch.

BUILDING APPS

The Internet is not the only place where you can cash in on the technology boom.

While using your smartphone or tablet, you've probably noticed all those programs that provide entertainment, make it easier to keep life organized, and help you keep in touch with family and friends.

These programs are better known as apps, and as more and more of our lives become tied to mobile technology, they are an increasingly great way for you to take advantage of your technical prowess.

What you'll need:

➡ A smartphone/tablet

➡ Some knowledge of coding

➡ An Integrated Development Environment (For Apple iOS this is XCode, for Android this is Eclipse and Android Studio, for Windows you will need the Windows Developer Account or Windows App Studio.)

HOW TO GET STARTED:

When you're considering what you want your app to do, think about your own experience with mobile devices.

Are you someone who loves playing games? Then perhaps you should use your passion and instincts to construct a game that others can enjoy.Would you be lost without the wonderful organization/productivity apps that exist? Build an app that will help people keep track of their time, appointments, activities, collections, exercise, etc.

Are you more into creating music or art? Get to work on something that will make it easier for you and your fellow artists to create anywhere, any time.

Once you know what kind of an app you want to build, check out the other offerings in this area. You'll not only get a sense of what is expected in terms of design, but you may see something that a popular app is missing. Work this "fix" into your own app, and you're golden. A small improvement is often all people need to try out something new!

If you build something that people find helpful, entertaining, or inspiring, the payoff can be tremendous.

One last thing before you get started. Make sure to familiarize yourself with the rules and guidelines of the operating system (Apple iOS, Android, Windows) you are using to design your app. It would be a shame to invest all that time and effort and then have your app rejected because it failed to meet some small specification.

BLOGGING

If you're more interested in the thought-provoking content on the Internet, you're still in a great position to make money. By starting a blog and writing about your interests and passions, you can build a devoted following that will draw people (and advertisers) to your site.

A blog is a great way to increase your visibility and expand your network. By sharing what you really care about, you'll make meaningful, lasting connections with people you otherwise would never have come into contact with.

So, even if the site does not become big enough to generate money, you may meet one person or several people who can help you out in the future!

HOW TO GET STARTED:

Create an interesting, unique, fun, and/or informative blog. You could create one about sports, current events, politics, entertainment, collectables, investing for young people . . . anything at all. Promote your site in places where your future readers will see it. One great place is in the comments and message board sections of websites that are similar to yours. Just be sure to keep your post short and on-topic. (No one likes a spammer!)

Start looking into ways where your site can make you money.

Many bloggers use ads, offer fans a "Donate!" button, or provide links to other products for sale.

Wordpress and Tumblr are both excellent places to house your blog. Take a look at the free designs both offer and see which ones catch your eye. These sites are so user friendly that once you decide on the right look, you'll be able to get up and start running in a matter of minutes. Post frequently so that people have a reason to check in often. "When you're starting out, three or four times a week should be enough. Once you garner a sizable audience, try to get something up at least once a day.

Don't feel like you always need to post an essay featuring a detailed analysis of last night's game or the most recent political debate. Displaying a song you've been addicted to lately, or a video clip of something that made you laugh is a great way to show your fans another side of you. Remember, this is supposed to be fun!

KID MILLIONAIRE PROFILE

As Ayesha Starns proves, blogs can be a stepping-stone toward much bigger things. Ayesha's love of the written word drove her to start a children's book review blog, which she then built into a well-respected network of book evaluations from other people her age. But she wasn't satisfied yet. Aided by the success of her site, Ayesha wrote the well-received book, "Buddy Bully" at just ten years of age! While she has moved on from her blog, Ayesha still remains involved in the literary world and works as an Author's Assistant, providing advice to those interested in publishing.

Here are a couple extra ideas:

- Set Up People's New Computers – For many people, the excitement of a new computer is overshadowed by the anxiety of installing the new software. If you're someone who has a facility with computers, step in and relieve all their fears. You'll be able to charge a good chunk of change for something that, as far as technology goes, is pretty simple.

- Managing Social Media Accounts – Take a look at the Facebook pages and Twitter accounts of the companies in your town. If you see one that hasn't been active in a while, contact the owner, explain that they're missing out on the considerable benefits social media has to offer, and offer to help out by providing timely engagement.

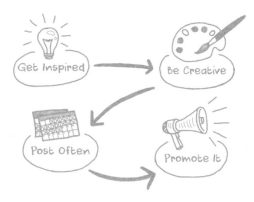

BLOGGING PLAN

MARKETING & SOCIAL MEDIA

WHAT YOU'LL LEARN:

- Utilizing YouTube
- The Golden Rule of Social Media
- Facebook
- Instagram
- Twitter
- Entrepreneur Apps
- Business Cards
- Re-selling for Profit

BUSINESS IDEAS COVERED:

✓ Re-selling online
✓ Selling your art & other crafts

ou already know that social media networks are great for keeping in touch with your friends and meeting new people, but they are also amazing marketing tools.

Consider Twitter's ability to put you in contact with your favorite movie stars, musicians and athletes. Well, this capability also provides you with a worldwide audience that is ready to receive your insights, analysis and recommendations.

Facebook not only provides you with a ready—made network, it also offers a free and very visible space for your business should you choose to build a page for it.

Instagram is an almost perfect marketing tool. By using your phone to photograph the things you find interesting and beautiful, you can bring people happiness that they won't soon forget, including what it was and who it came from. It's almost too good to be true. A presence on social media will make you, and your business, visible when people enter either into a search engine. This visibility not only makes it easier for people to find you, it also inspires trust, helping people see that you are someone who is open, honest and passionate. In other words, you are someone worth doing business with.

This is the way the world, and business is heading. Make sure you're not left behind!

▶ UTILIZE YOUTUBE

Of all the online communities, YouTube is the best opportunity to make some money and build a following. Due to the number of devoted users and how easy it is for them to share the content they love, YouTube is a tremendously powerful outlet. So if you're charming, and good in front of the camera, it's definitely worth trying out.

Star in your own YouTube series! If you become popular, you can get paid through their Partnership program. (One quick thing: You will need one of your parents' email addresses if you're under 18.)

Love to cook? By filming yourself in the kitchen and showing people how to make some of your favorite dishes, you can cash in on the current "foodie" craze!

If you have serious gaming skills, it's worth capturing them on video. Assassin's Creed, Game of Thrones, Halo, Minecraft and a number of others are currently very popular. Any program associated with them is sure to attract a ton of eyeballs!

Become an educator. Do you know a foolproof way to start a campfire? An awesome method for folding T-shirts? Film yourself doing it. You'll be amazed by how many people need your help.

Do you love movies? Get some friends together and write a short film. Even if the product doesn't catch on and go viral, you'll have a blast and gain useful experience.

YouTube is also a great way for musicians to build a following. Write a few songs, record them with a video camera/smartphone and put them up for others to enjoy. You'll become increasingly more comfortable performing, and put yourself in a position to be discovered. These videos will also serve as a perfect audition tape when you are trying to get live gigs!

THE GOLDEN RULE OF SOCIAL MEDIA

There's a rule that successful social media entrepreneurs follow: 80% of the time you want to provide value and 20% of the time you want to be selling your product.

The 80/20 rule recognizes that, in this day and age, people are bombarded with advertisements and offers everywhere they look online. You don't want to become part of this crowd. You will either be tuned out or grouped in with the despised horde of annoying online advertisers.

In this instance, providing value means pushing content that people will find helpful, connecting people with other folks in your industry, and providing insightful questions and commentary on your peers' online offerings. Doing this allows you to position yourself as a knowledgeable authority in your chosen field and someone people can turn to when in need.

If you can reach this point, you won't have to hound people into purchasing your product or services. They'll know where to go when they're looking for a solution!

THE BIG THREE

If you're going to focus your advertising push on social media, here are a few tips for the three major outlets.

FACEBOOK

On Facebook, and for all social media, you always want to be thinking about how to increase your reach (the number of "followers" or "friends") and how to reward those people who are already in your network.

To do this with your business' Facebook page, offer discounts and special promotions to those who give you a "like" or a positive review. Deals like this will help increase awareness of your business and create considerable goodwill toward it. These two elements are crucial when trying to distinguish your business from the rest and establish a foothold.

Another helpful way to provide value and increase fondness and awareness is to start a Facebook group. By creating a space where people in your particular field, or young entrepreneurs in your area, can come together and share their challenges, triumphs and content, you have an opportunity to build incredibly valuable relationships. The advantage of groups is that they connect you to people who both understand your world and have their own unique perspective on it. All of a sudden, you'll have access to experts in an area where you may struggle. Or to people so overloaded with work that they toss a job or two your way. You will find individuals who provide excellent support and guidance during those times when you're struggling. And, in addition to all the business benefits, you may discover that you share a few other interests with these people and find life-long friends.

Once you have an established business page with a decent-sized group of supporters and devotees, you will be able to take advantage of Facebook advertisements. These have become highly effective means of increasing awareness and improving sales. Because of the considerable data created by Facebook's large membership, your ads have the ability to target users according to a variety of factors, such as those who have liked one of your competitors' business pages or people who live in your town. This will ensure that your message hits its mark.

INSTAGRAM

 Instagram is a godsend for marketing small businesses, particularly people involved with creative endeavors.

It provides insight on the beautiful creations captured as well as its creator. People on Instagram tend to form extremely close attachments to the accounts that they follow.

But first, you have to get those followers! One easy way to do this is to offer periodic giveaways, where you post a photo of a special, one-of-a-kind product and provide those following you a chance to win it in a drawing. All they have to do to gain entry into the drawing is like your post and tag five people who are not already following your account. These drawings will bring your work (and your awesome generosity) to the attention of a whole new crew of folks! And if they like what they see, the rapid growth of your fan base easily makes up for the free giveaway.

Another proven method of driving up interest on Instagram are "Instagram Followers Only" sales, where you offer discounts and exclusive, special edition items to those individuals fortunate enough to make up your following. Lured in by the chance to take part in

 these incredible sales, people will pay close attention to your every post. Not only that, they'll be so eager to share this opportunity with their friends that they'll urge them to get onboard, giving you a team of passionate marketers for free!

TWITTER

 Able to disseminate information and connect individuals like nothing else, Twitter has zoomed to the fore of the changing media landscape. Unfortunately, the tremendous power it offers also makes it easy to get lost in the sea of individuals who are eager to utilize it for themselves.

In order to distinguish yourself from this noisy mass, it's smart to take your time, sit back and listen before you begin to engage. Just because it's easy to share every thought you have doesn't mean that you should. The goal is not just to share, but to have effective and impactful content .

Hang back and listen to those you want to interact with. Doing this not only gives you a sense of the issues they are trying to find solutions for, it also tells you how they want to converse, and what the best method of approach is. Perhaps they frequently respond to whoever comments or they engage with members who have posted an article they liked. Whatever their preference, you can only get a sense of this by paying close attention to their tweets.

While you are listening, you also want to be building a carefully cultivated timeline of your own. Before they follow you most people will check in to see if your insightful/educational tweet was representative of your typical offering or an anomaly. In order to ensure that it's the former, ask yourself these three questions before posting a tweet: 1) Does it bring up an issue that people should know about? 2) Do you have quality analysis/thoughts to add? 3) Would you say it in front of a room filled with strangers? If the answer to each is yes to all three of them, you can feel comfortable posting.

One last tip for Twitter: people are more inclined to engage with a video than an article. So, when you can, tailor your tweets to take advantage of this tendency!

HELPFUL APPS FOR
THE ENTREPRENEUR

➡ Buffer

Instead of logging into each social media platform and posting a new piece of information separately, this app allows you to view your posts for every app in one place and create a posting schedule for all of them.

➡ Brand24:

Trying to get a quick read on your company's public perception? Brand24 aggregates what has been said online and also keeps tabs on your competition. This app's vigilance allows you to focus on doing your work, alerting you to provide timely engagement when needed.

➡ Pocket:

If you're on the go, it's easy to lose track of things and miss out on an opportunity. This app helps you stay on top of what you encounter out in the world, whether it be an article you want to post later on or an important document somebody sends your way.

➡ Nuzzel:

If you are going to make Facebook and/or Twitter a big part of your marketing/networking strategy, then this app is a must-have. It helps you organize the stories shared by your friends into links and allows you to add influencers that can help tailor them to your specific needs.

➡ Babbly:

This app is for those interested in going viral. All you have to do is post a link to whatever you want to promote! Babbly takes over from there, promoting the content within its own community.

IDEAS ON BUSINESS CARDS

When you're deciding on business cards there are two goals. First, you want to provide people with your essential information. And second, you want something that's striking, something that will make people stop and take notice.

Those may seem obvious, but achieving them is anything but easy. To see what we mean, take a look at Moo.com or VistaPrint. After a half-hour, your head will be swimming with possibilities! So here are a couple of tips that will help you navigate the numerous options and make the choice that is right for you.

At the moment, the most popular setup is to have an intriguing image, graphic or design on the front and place your information on the back. Should you choose this option, don't get hung up trying to find something that perfectly encapsulates what your business is. Instead, try to find something that communicates who you are to the individual encountering the card.

This will depend on the type of work that you do, and your interests. Do you own a landscaping company with a focus on planting flowers? Search for something that is sunny and lively. Did you start a computer repair business because you love the precision computers require? Think about going with a simple design that expresses this passion.

As we said, you want the front of the card to be striking. However, this does not mean overly flashy or obnoxious. You want a look that intrigues people not something that makes people write you off.

Keep in mind that a business card is not just a means of providing people with your contact information. It also signals what an interaction with you will be like. When you are sorting through candidates for the front of your card, ask yourself which ones are representative of your personality and which ones cry out for people's attention. Focusing on the designs that are in line with your attitude will keep you from making a loud, potentially harmful choice.

If you do want to stand out, one way to distinguish yourself without being annoying is through the shape of your card. As you probably know, the traditional shape of a business card is a rectangle. However, in recent years, companies have been offering square business cards and business cards with rounded edges. This small difference is just enough to signal that you are unique and may draw the attention of someone who is so used to the traditional rectangle that they've become numb to it!

Once you've drawn them in with the front of the card, you want to convey your information as quickly and as simply as you can on the back. But simplicity does not mean that less thought is required.

When deciding on the design for the back of your card, you will need to think about these two things: "What is my preferred means of communication?" and "What methods are my customers likely to favor?"

These two questions will help you determine what makes it onto the back of your card and the order it is displayed. For instance, let's say that you do not like talking on the phone and are much more comfortable interacting via e-mail. If that's the case, you want to make sure your business card signals this desire and places your e-mail address in a higher position than your telephone number. Or, if you are in an industry where people's primary interactions occur online, it makes sense to have your web address, Twitter, Instagram or Facebook handle in a prominent position.

If this seems like a lot of pressure, don't worry. A business card is not a magic bullet that will have people begging you to take their money. It's just a means of providing a brief introduction and a way to continue the conversation.

But, as we all know, first impressions are often the most important thing.

FRONT

BACK

OTHER TECH-RELATED ENDEAVORS

➡ **Animation commissions:** Everybody loves animation but very few people realize how easy it is to learn. If you swoop in to meet the demand, you can charge up to a dollar-per-second making personalized animations for people! For those who need an introduction, a simple program like Scratch is a good place to start. If you're artistically inclined and advanced, seek out DeviantArt.

➡ **Create PowerPoint presentations:** Even though originality and appearance are everything in a presentation, people who present with PowerPoints are often too busy to concern themselves with how they look and end up going with the same old, tired approach. If you're into design, offer your services to these poor souls! All you have to do is turn the information they provide into an attractive set of slides. Interested? Websites like Upwork list these available jobs, and many other kinds of freelance work.

RE-SELL ONLINE FOR PROFIT

The Internet is a great place to shop and has a number of resale outlets. Make some quick cash by selling items online, or make a steady income by selling other people's things!

What you'll need:

➡ A computer with an internet connection

➡ A digital camera/iPhone

➡ Boxes and shipping supplies (packing tape, mailing labels, etc.)

HOW TO GET STARTED:

Start with toys you don't use, video games you don't play, or movies, CDs and records you're tired of. Look them up on used resale sites such as Amazon and eBay. How much can you get for them? For now, don't bother listing the items that are only worth a dollar or two.

When listing an item, be sure to mention any dents, scratches, tears, scuffs, or markings. One bad review can derail your career as an online seller. Since a good reputation is a must, be entirely upfront. You don't want your customers to have any unpleasant surprises when they open up their shipment, Keep an eye out for yard sales and at thrift stores to find items that you know will sell quickly (and for a nice profit). Cool sunglasses and vintage, designer clothing is usually available if you've got the patience to pick through everything, and they go for a pretty penny online.

Once you get the hang of the business and want to expand, you can begin listing and shipping items. (For a commission, of course!)

Be careful about shipping and handling. Find out in advance how much it will cost to ship each item you list, otherwise you might charge too little and end up losing money. And make sure you have the materials to properly package the item when you put it up for sale. Shipping an item out quickly is a huge factor when people are considering what kind of a review to give you. The Internet moves fast so always be prepared and don't drag your feet!

CREDIT CARD

8811 6G12 1234
03/20-02/40
KID MILLIONAIRE

BUY

THE ARTISTE

If you are an artistic individual who is constantly creating, the Internet can be as good as a gallery space. Thanks to sites like Etsy, CafePress and Zazzle, the myth of the starving artist is so last millennium. Now it's easy to use your inventive abilities to start a successful business.

What you'll need:

➡ Art supplies

➡ Access to a computer with a scanner

HOW TO GET STARTED:

The goal is to sell your work, but of course you must first create work to sell. Give some thought into what you like to draw, paint, or photograph, and what pieces of your past work have gotten the best responses from other people. Once you know what's going to make you and others happy, you can get to work!

After you've created your pieces, you have to think commercially. Buyers sometimes purchase framed or mounted art, but they're much more likely to buy posters, coffee mugs, bumper stickers, T-shirts, postcards, and journals that have art displayed on it. Think about which items will be the best medium for the kind of work you do.

Once you've found the best way to display your art, start investing in your business by having the items made. (Remember: the more you order at once, the less you are paying upfront per item!) Find local stores and gift shops that would be willing to buy them from you, or you can try to sell them online.

CafePress takes a big cut of your profit, but it also takes the burden of manufacturing and selling your items off of your plate. All you have to do is spread the word and they do the rest. Zazzle gives you a choice on how involved you want to be. They can manufacture what you design or you can do the manufacturing and use their site to sell your pieces and keep your orders organized. Etsy gives you a space to display your items and charges a low transaction fee for the items that you do sell, but leaves you completely in charge of manufacturing and shipping.

As you can see, you've got plenty of options! If you're interested in selling your work take a close look at each website and see which one is best for you.

ONLINE SALES SUCCESS STORIES

When it comes to selling online, Azriel Kimmel is wise beyond his years. At just thirteen, he buys discounted items at various stores and then sells them on eBay for a profit. The key to Azriel's success is thinking big. Two years ago, he saw a popular video game marked down for just $5 in a store and, realizing he'd be able to sell it for twice as much online, bought all 65 copies. Azriel

then did the same thing during a Black Friday sale, buying seven $85 netbooks and selling them for $150 a piece on eBay.

If you're inspired by Azriel's success but aren't sure where to start, ask your parents for help! I know of one mother who helped her 5-year-old sell his Fisher Price GeoTrax toys on Craigslist for $120!

BUILDING A BIGGER ENTERPRISE

WHAT YOU'LL LEARN:

- How to Find the Best Advertising Method
- The Increasing Value of Email Addresses
- Knowing When It's Time to Expand
- Finding a Space for Yourself
- How to Break in New Employees

EXPANDING YOUR REACH AND ADVERTISING

While the Internet and social media are key to building awareness, they still take a backseat to direct contact with people. Throughout this book we've tried to emphasize the importance of interpersonal communication, and it still remains vital when you're trying to grow. If someone feels strongly enough about your work that they're willing to voice their support, chances are very high that someone else will take their recommendation.

Another way to contact people directly and expand your reach is through email. Every time you perform a service for someone, make sure you ask for an email address. Place the addresses you receive into a contact list in your own mail account. You'll then be able to reach out any time you're offering a special deal, a discount, or providing a new service. An email address keeps a line of communication open and it also keeps you in people's minds.

Remember, it's not just the people you've done work for that make up your audience, it's also all the people they know. By sending out periodic emails to your customers, some of them may forward it to a friend or colleague who is looking for someone like you.

An email list has become an extremely powerful method of advertising. But use this power wisely. People don't like being bombarded with emails from one sender, so make each one of your messages count. And if someone asks to be removed from your email list please honor the request.

TRADITIONAL ADVERTISING

Creating business cards is always a good idea, so visit Vistaprint or Moo to choose something that's eye-catching and make sure your name, the name of your business, your phone number, email and social media info is included. Once you've received your cards, hand them out to the people you do work for and those that show an interest in hiring you.

You can also tack your business cards up onto bulletin boards at coffee shops and cafés around your town. If you choose a snappy design, someone who is waiting for a table just might stumble upon your card and contact you!

Running a lawn care, house painting or other home improvement service? Create signs advertising your business and ask your customers if you can put a sign up in their yard. This way the people driving by will know who is responsible for the impressive work they're seeing, and understand with whom they should contact when they want something done at their own house.

The classic avenues of advertising: radio, television and newspapers are tricky, since they tend to require lots of capital. Not only are they expensive, their influence is dwindling as more and more information and entertainment moves onto the Internet. Focusing on building your web presence will not only be cheaper, there's a good chance it will also prove more effective.

EXPENSES, SPACE AND EMPLOYEES

At the start, it is important to limit your business' expenses as much as possible. If you aren't careful, there's a chance you might be making far less than your time is worth, or even losing money!

But there comes a time when it is wise to invest what seems like a considerable sum into your business. The old saying, "You need to spend money to make money" will prove to be true.

It can be confusing and scary, but it's also an incredible position to be in. To have brought your business to a point, where shelling out money will bring back much more in return, is a tremendous accomplishment. So before you dive in take a step back and appreciate all the great work you've done!

How do you know when the time is right to expand? Pay attention to demand. If you find yourself having to turn down jobs because you already have too many other work-related commitments, you may want to think about expanding.

This is one occasion when having too much on your plate is a good thing! Building your business to this point means that you've paid close attention to what people want, so why would you stop now? If the demand is considerable and you are unable to meet it by yourself, you may want to consider hiring other people, renting a space, and moving into more of an advisory/managerial role.

RENTING A SPACE

Is your business based around your creativity? Does it require extremely close attention? Then you may want to consider renting a space. This way, you'll be able to focus and won't be interrupted by questions from your parents or noise from your younger siblings.

Office space is usually pretty affordable. But beware! Go over the lease carefully and try to leave yourself with an out if you can. (It may even be worth paying a little bit more in rent if you can secure a month-to-month lease.) You don't want to be left holding the bag if the space becomes unnecessary or proves to be too much money.

There are also more and more shared office spaces popping up. These are spaces where you can rent a desk and be surrounded by other entrepreneurs, or rent an office and be by yourself. If there is one of these spaces in your area and you're thinking about getting some outside space, check it out! These can be excellent places to meet new people and are much cheaper than renting an office all by yourself.

HIRING EMPLOYEES

Are any of your friends intrigued by all the money you're making? Are any of them looking for work? You may want to think about bringing them on as employees. Think about it: If you can cut two lawns or paint two houses at the same time, you just doubled the amount of money you have coming in.

The most important thing is to find people who can uphold the high standard of work that you've set. You definitely don't want to try to expand your business and then hire people whose performance ends up eating away at your profits.

So be careful! Try to be with your new hires during the first few jobs that they do. Call it a training period and watch them closely. If they are going to be more harmful than helpful, you'll be able to tell pretty quickly.

THE PUP OF WALL STREET

WHAT YOU'LL LEARN:

- Compound Interest is Your Best Friend
- The Importance of Diversifying
- Your Investment Options
- How to Take Risks Without Going Broke
- The Very Best Investment Available

BUSINESS IDEAS COVERED:

✓ Compound interest
✓ Accounts, bonds, cds, etc
✓ Real estate
✓ Mutual funds
✓ IRAs
✓ Stocks
✓ Startups

ongratulations! You now have an income, your own spending money, and even some savings (both short and long term). You're already miles ahead of most people your age!

So what now? You can call it a day, or you can use the power of compound interest to set yourself up for life. All you have to do is . . . INVEST!

SPOILER ALERT: We're going to start throwing around some big words. There will even be a bit of math. But since you've made it this far, you're clearly a sharp individual. And if you can learn this stuff now, you'll be in great shape for the future.

THE MIRACLE OF COMPOUND INTEREST

Do you ever feel like you're missing out on all the fun because you're not an adult yet? Like there are all these things you can't do just because of your age?

Well, in this country we have something where your youth puts you at an advantage. In fact, the younger you are, the more incredible this investment is. Intrigued?

Suppose someone had invested $1,000 for you on the day you were born. If the interest rate on this initial investment was 10% every year, and you didn't touch that money until your sixty-fifth birthday, how much money would you have?

$1,100? $65,000?

Try $490,370.73!

Sound pretty good? You're halfway to one million dollars and you didn't have to do a thing.

Compound interest did all the work for you. If this seems like magic, that's because it kind of is.How is this possible? Let's break it down:

On your first birthday, your $1,000 earned $100 in interest, which was added to your account.

On your second birthday, your $1,100.00 earned $110.00 in interest, which was again added to your account.

Did you see what happened? Your interest earned interest! That's what compound interest is.

On your fifth birthday, you had $1,610.51. On your tenth birthday you now had $2,593.74. Crazy, right? You gained almost $1,000 between when you were five and ten! And after that, it really gets wild:

At fifteen years old you would have $4,177.25.

At twenty years old you would have $6,727.50.

At thirty years old you would have $17,449.40.

At forty years old you would have $45,259.26.

At fifty years old you would have $117,390.85.

At sixty years old you would have $304,481.64.

And then $490,370.73 on your sixty-fifth birthday! That's a whole lot of video games! We haven't even talked about what would happen if someone added just $100 to that account every year ($979,741.45). Or if instead of earning 10% every year, the account earned 12% ($1,581,872.49).

Now it's easy to see that the younger you are when you begin saving, the more time compound interest has to work its magic, and the less you have to do to become a millionaire!

DIVERSIFYING YOUR INVESTMENTS

Most people's introduction to investing is an interest-bearing savings account. While this is a good place to start, you don't want to stay there forever. It's always smart to diversify your investments.

Diversifying helps cover all your bases. You'll make sure you don't miss out on something when it is booming, and avoid being harmed too much if a particular investment bottoms out.

A good diversification strategy is to keep a bulk of your money in safe, stable investments. These could be a standard savings account, a money market account, government bonds, CDs, and IRAs. Once you have this solid foundation, devote a small amount (5% or 10% or whatever you're comfortable with) to high-risk, high-reward investments such as stocks and promising businesses that are just starting out. This way, you'll be sure to keep building your nest egg while also giving yourself an opportunity to strike it rich if one of your longshots pays off. Until you turn eighteen and can invest in your own name, you may need your parents or guardian to set up a custodial account to invest in some of these options. But since you're being so forward thinking and responsible, getting them to cooperate shouldn't be a problem!

INSTANT MONEY: ACCOUNTS, BONDS, CDS, ETC.

Just like business ideas, different kinds of investments have different levels of risk. The safest options—like government bonds, CDs, and money market accounts—also have the lowest level of interest. Your money is pretty safe, but it's not going to grow very much.

Other, slightly riskier options—like corporate bonds, mutual funds, and real estate—will have more variation. They'll go up, then down, and up again. But if you can remain patient, sit tight and let the market work its long-term magic, they will usually reward you with a higher return than the safer options.

Stocks are the riskiest option, and if you want to try your hand at them, prepare yourself for a wild ride featuring exceptional highs and crushing lows. Some stocks are safer than others, but none of them are guaranteed to make you money.

Since investing can be overwhelming, we're going to slow it down a bit and provide a brief introduction to each of your options.

LOW RISK

1. Government Bonds

"Buying a bond" is just another way of saying that you are lending money. In this case, it's to your local government (these are called municipal bonds) or your federal government (these are called treasury bonds).

Your state and local governments use the money from municipal bonds to build schools, hospitals, highways, and many other important things. The federal government uses the money from treasury bonds to help pay off the national debt.

In both cases, you buy a bond for less than the bond is worth. (Some cost as little as $25 or $50; some cost much more.) Then, once the bond matures (which is another way of saying that they are ready to pay you back, with interest), you can cash the bond in for its full value!

Different bonds mature at different rates. Treasury bonds mature in a year or less (but you pay less interest). Municipal bonds may take as long as thirty years but your patience will be rewarded. The longer a bond takes to mature, the more interest you will earn.

Interested in starting to diversify with a few government bonds? You can buy them at most banks.

2. CDs

CD stands for "certificate of deposit," a.k.a. lending money to a bank. Unlike bonds, which you're allowed to sell back before they mature, you have to hold on to CDs for the amount of time you have agreed. This could be anywhere from a month to five years.

CDs are a very safe investment: Even if the bank goes out of business your money is guaranteed by the federal government (up to $100,000!). Because CDs are safe, the interest they offer is pretty low, but they are a good option if you're willing to put up a nice chunk of change.

3. Money Market Accounts

A money market deposit account is just like a checking or savings account at a bank. The only difference is that you have to keep a larger amount of money in your account and you can't withdraw as often as you would be able to with a checking or savings account.

However, the interest rates offered are higher than your regular savings account. And like CDs, your money is insured by the federal government.

SOME RISK

1. Corporate Bonds

Big companies are just like the government: they're eager to borrow your money! You may be familiar with some of them: Disney, IBM, and Nike are just a few companies where you can lend your money.

You will probably earn more interest from a corporate bond than you would from a government bond. But beware! If the company goes out of business, your money may disappear with them.

2. Real Estate

That's right, you could own property! Buying a house or even land is usually a very good investment, but it will cost you thousands of dollars (sometimes hundreds of thousands), and you will have to pay taxes on the property every year.

One way to invest in real estate without actually owning anything is through a kind of mutual fund called a real estate investment trust.

3. Mutual Funds

A mutual fund is a combination of stock investments that allow other, smaller investors (like you) to "buy" a share and receive a piece of the profits.

Mutual funds are less risky than stocks because each fund has money invested in multiple companies. This means your investment is protected even if one company in the fund is doing poorly or goes out of business. As long as a majority of the companies in the mutual fund are doing well, you can withstand a few bumps in the road.

However, you've probably heard all about the stock market occasionally getting itself into big trouble. If it's big enough, it could mean trouble for your mutual fund investments.

4. IRAs

An IRA, which is similar to a mutual fund but offers better tax benefits, is often the best bang for your buck. They are such an effective means of saving that the amount you can place into them is capped at a few thousand dollars. A Roth IRA also provides some flexibility and allows you to remove the principal (the money you initially put in) any time you want. There are several different kinds of IRAs and each has a unique tax benefit and structure, so take a look and see which one works for you.

LOTS OF RISK
. . . .

1. Stocks

Buying stock in a company is just another way of saying that you are now "part-owner" of that company. So if you purchased stock in PepsiCo, Apple Inc., and HJ Heinz, you would own a piece of

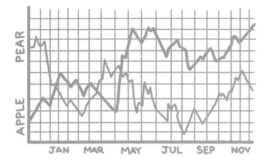

the companies that make Pepsi, iPads, and the ketchup in your refrigerator. Imagine that!

However, you need to proceed with caution. You can learn to read how a stock did today, or how well it has done over time, and you can look over reports from the company to its stockholders. But at the end of the day, the stock market is highly unpredictable. Many an investor has made a fortune and then lost it because they thought they had everything figured out.

There have been numerous great books written about investing in stocks. If you are interested in learning more, you should check out *The Intelligent Investor* or *The Little Book of Common Sense Investing*.

2. Start-Ups

Getting a business started is very exciting, but also very stressful. In order to relieve some of this stress, certain people will seek out investors early on. Think of it as the stock market on a smaller scale. You can invest and become a part-owner or make a deal to receive a share of future profits.

However, you should always remember that most new businesses fail, even those that seem like they can't miss. While an early investment can pay off big—Mike Markkula, who invested in Apple when Steve Jobs and Steve Wozniak were running it out of a garage, certainly struck gold—it's still pretty rare. It's fine to make small wagers on a few companies, but you don't want to have too much of your money tied up in them.

THE VERY BEST INVESTMENT

Money is not everything, and while it can position you well for the future, it should never be the measure of your own worth. In fact, the best possible thing you can do to ensure a life of adventure, happiness, and financial security is to . . . invest in yourself!

Compound interest doesn't only work on money. All the knowledge and experience you are gaining now will make you a much more capable, confident person later on.

Invest your time in the things you love to do. If there's a summer sports camp you feel can help your athletic dreams come true, don't be afraid to step away from your thriving business. If your volunteer experiences at a hospital made you realize that you want to be a doctor or a nurse, don't hesitate to invest in college even if you have to take out loans to do it.

REMEMBER:

YOU ARE
THE BEST
INVESTMENT
YOU CAN MAKE!

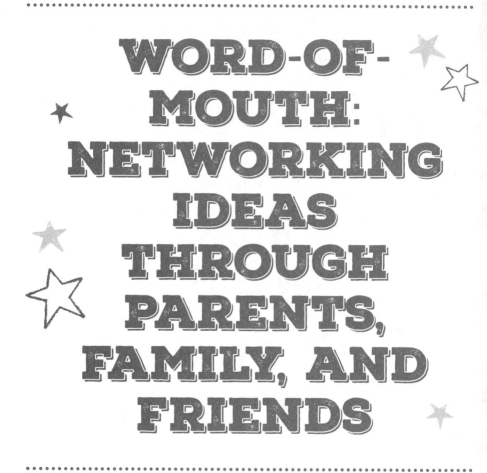

WORD-OF-MOUTH: NETWORKING IDEAS THROUGH PARENTS, FAMILY, AND FRIENDS

WHAT YOU'LL LEARN:

- Advertising through networking
- Mentorship and guidance

If you're looking to go out on your own, but are worried that you won't be able to get any customers, don't forget about the powerful network right in front of your face: your family and friends! Let them know about your plans. Ask them to send an email to their contact list announcing the service you're offering or to mention your business to their co-workers and friends.

All of a sudden you've created a considerable amount of awareness about your venture. All you had to do was ask for help from those who are naturally inclined to want to do so!

This is an important lesson for any entrepreneur/small business owner. Just because you've decided to go out on your own, doesn't mean you have to do everything yourself. You still need to rely on those closest to you, especially in the beginning when there is so much to do. The sooner you can ask for help, the better chance your business has of succeeding!

Email and word-of-mouth are not the only ways to increase the buzz about your venture. If you know that a member of your family or one of your friends has a large party scheduled, and your business can be displayed in that environment, offer up your services for free.

Whether it be designing invitations, photographing the festivities, landscaping the yard beforehand, baking cupcakes, or decorating, a party is an excellent chance to grab the attention of a lot of people who would otherwise never be exposed to your talents. So keep your ears perked up for any opportunities to shine. It just might give you plenty to celebrate!

FIND A MENTOR

Another important part to navigating the choppy waters of starting your own business is finding a mentor. Take a look at the people closest to you. If any are small business owners, or used to be, contact them. Tell them about the plans for your venture and ask if you can meet to talk with them for advice or future guidance.

While it is preferable to have someone with experience in the industry you are interested in entering, it is not essential. The most important thing is finding someone you feel comfortable with and who possesses enough business sense to shine light on those areas that you, as a novice, cannot see.

Use the first meeting to get a sense of their outlook and judge whether they have the ability to inspire you. You'll be able to tell pretty quickly if this is someone you can learn from. Once you get this sense, ask if they would be willing to talk every other week or once a month.

You may be wondering: "Why would anyone want to give up their valuable time to help someone like me?" There's a good chance they've gotten to where they are because someone did the same thing for them. By helping a young, inexperienced entrepreneur succeed, they've paid off their debt and helped keep the cycle going!

TRAINING   MOTIVATION   ADVICE   SUCCESS

MENTORING

GOAL   SUPPORT   COACHING   DIRECTION

MILLIONAIRE KID STORIES

WHAT YOU'LL LEARN:

- About Web Designers
- About YouTube stars
- About Software Developers
- About Fashion Designers
- About Philanthropists
- About Chefs and Cooks
- And more!

CHRISTIAN OWENS OF MAC BUNDLE BOX

Christian taught himself web design at an early age. He caught on so quickly that he started his first design company at just fourteen. That's impressive by itself, but in less than two years Christian already made his first million! Like his hero Steve Jobs, Christian didn't rest after his earlier accomplishments. He used his skills and connections to negotiate with manufacturers and distributors, and put together a discounted applications bundle for Apple's OS X. Christian's *Mac Bundle Box* has since made him millions.

The lesson: Always be on the lookout for ways to save people money. If you can offer a lower price on something they already purchase, you're in great shape.

EMIL MOTYCKA OF MOTYCKA ENTERPRISES

Like many kids, Emil started his entrepreneurial career with a lawn mowing business at the age of eight. Where he separated himself from other kids mowing lawns, was by taking out a loan for $8,000 when he was just thirteen. He used the loan to purchase a commercial lawn mower that pushed his business to the next level. By eighteen, Emil formed *Motycka Enterprises* and went on to make well over $100,000 that summer. Thanks to his courage and his vision, he's now making millions.

The lesson: If you can provide people with a higher level of service, you'll never lack for work.

EVAN OF EVANTUBE

At the age of nine, Evan had the bright idea to start a YouTube channel called *EvanTube*. Thanks to more than a million subscribers and the help of his father, he now brings in approximately $1.3 million a year. How did he do it? By reviewing toys and other fun items kids his age are into! If you have the ambition and drive, you can get rich talking about the topics you would normally discuss for nothing with your friends.

The lesson: Always pay attention to the interests of the people around you. If you can tap in to what people love in a different and engaging way, you could find yourself in Evan's shoes.

CAMERON JOHNSON OF CHEERS AND TEARS

Cameron's start was as modest as possible: he made the invitations for a party his parents were throwing. Some of the guests were so taken with the quality of the invitations they not only asked Cameron to make invites for them, they also paid him for it! Inspired by this early success, Cameron founded *Cheers and Tears* at eleven and quickly moved on to software development and online advertising. By high school, he was making approximately $300,000 to $400,000 a month! Not a bad return for helping out mom and dad!

The lesson: To do something well is one thing, but to take it to another level is something else. Never be afraid to trust in your ability and try something new. It just might make you a millionaire!

ADAM HILDRETH OF DUBIT AND CRISP

Adam was named one of the United Kingdom's 20 Richest Teens in 2004 at the age of nineteen. When he was just fourteen years old, he had created the popular UK social networking site for teenagers called *Dubit*, and became a millionaire by the age of sixteen. He then went on to create *Crisp*, a company that helps protect kids from online predators.

The lesson: Keep an eye out for popular trends and try to create your own niche within it. Also be on the lookout for problems in need of solutions. As Adam's example illustrates, both can pay off in a big way.

MOZIAH BRIDGES OF MO'S BOWS

At the age of nine, Moziah started a bow tie company that exploded almost immediately and has brought him a very handsome $150,000 a year. Today, Moziah has several employees, has been featured in several popular magazines, and even appeared on the current en-  trepreneurial TV show *Shark Tank*! Moziah, who obviously knows a thing or two about dressing for success, is now hard at work on a full clothing line!

The lesson: Starting a successful business is a tremendous achievement, but don't let early success stop you in your tracks.

GEOFF, DAVE, & CATHERINE COOK OF MYYEARBOOK

. . . .

Before Facebook, these three siblings started *myYearbook*, a social networking site based on the school(s) you attended. Instead of focusing on college, like Facebook, they decided to concentrate on grade school after they moved to a new town and wanted to make friends. Thanks to many others who shared this same desire, the site exploded. After six years the Cooks sold their site to Quepasa Corps for $100 million. There's nothing elementary about that.

The lesson: Instead of pouting when things don't go your way, try to create a solution! If you can maintain a positive outlook, your own life is often the biggest creative spark you need.

SANJAY & SHAVRAN KUMARAN OF GODIMENSIONS

. . . .

Sanjay and Shavran, twelve and fourteen respectively, have developed several gaming apps. Thanks to more than 35,000 downloads, they've been able to turn their creations into a corporation! Sanjay and Shavran, who developed the popular *Catch Me Cop* app, offer their apps for free and make money exclusively through advertising. When they're not tied up with their corporation, these two visionaries speak at events and conferences, offering people advice on how to make their ideas a reality.

The lesson: When what you love and what you're good at are the same, there's absolutely nothing keeping you from the top.

FARRHAD ACIDWALLA OF ROCKSTAH MEDIA

Farrhad founded the marketing agency Rockstah Media at just sixteen. But he didn't do it alone. *Rockstah* consisted of 20 employees from around the world. And while Farrhad's vision is what powered the company, he credits his entire team for its success, saying: "My team is the backbone of my company."

The lesson: You can't do it all on your own. Building a strong team is a necessity if you are going to make your business an overwhelming success.

ROBERT NAY OF THE BUBBLE BALL APP

Thanks to the unbelievable success of his *Bubble Ball* game, Robert made more than $2 million in two weeks. Not bad considering that he was just fourteen at the time! His game, which continues to be one of the most popular games in Apple's App Store, has been downloaded over 16 million times and featured on *Good Morning America.* But Robert hasn't let fame and fortune go to his head. To this day he continues to develop apps with his company, *Nay Games*.

The lesson: Overnight, runaway success shouldn't be the goal. But it can only happen if you have something to put out there so get going!

NICK D'ALOISIO OF SUMMLY

Nick became one of the world's youngest self-made millionaires when Yahoo! purchased his company, Summly, for $30 million in 2013. Summly became the Yahoo! News Digest and Nick became the Wall Street Journal's "Innovator of the Year." He has also been included in TIME Magazine's "Time 100" and became the youngest person to receive a round of venture capital in technology from the Hong Kong billionaire Li Ka-Shing.

The lesson: Age isn't going to keep you from being a success. If you have something good enough smart people are going to pay attention, no matter how young you are.

LEANNA ARCHER OF LEANNA'S HAIR

As a nine-year-old, Leanna was already bottling and selling her own hair pomade, using secret recipes from her great-grandmother. Having expanded to an entire line of hair products, Leanna's company brings in over $100,000 annually and her net worth is over $3 million. However, she doesn't keep all that money to herself. She also founded the Leanna Archer Education Foundation, which helps provide basic needs, including education, to 200 Haitian children each day.

The lesson: Always try to give back. Money can make a huge difference in people's lives so do your best to make sure it's not just in your own!

FRASER DOHERTY OF SUPERJAM

Using his grandmother's recipes, Fraser got his start
by selling homemade jam to his neighbors at the age of
fourteen. Within two years, his jams were in such demand
that he dropped out of school to work on his product full-
time. Eventually, Fraser's jams caught the attention of
a high-end supermarket chain in the UK. They offered to
carry his product in all 184 of its stores. In order to ramp
up production, Fraser took out a $9,000 loan to cover the cost of
increased factory time. Through this small gamble and his own hard
work, SuperJam hit $1.2 million in sales in 2009.

Lesson: If the demand for your product presents you with a life-
altering opportunity, don't let anything stand in your way.

ADAM HORWITZ OF MOBILE MONOPOLY AND YEPTEXT

Adam was driven from a very early age. He set a goal to create
a million-dollar company by the time he turned twenty-one and
launched a start-up website at the age of fifteen. While his first few
failed to gain traction, his Mobile Monopoly app, which teaches users
how to capitalize on mobile market leads, made him a handsome
six-figure profit. Still short of his goal, Adam used the money from
this to fund YepText, a text to advertise services for businesses, and
Young & Boss, a social network for young CEOs.

Lesson: Don't be afraid of failure. If you have drive and believe in
yourself, you'll be able to learn from your mistakes instead of being
discouraged by them.

TYLER DIKMAN OF COOLTRONICS

Starting out in the classic trades of lawn mowing, lemonade stands, and babysitting, Tyler got his first computer at age ten. He took it apart and studied its mechanics and was soon repairing computers for his teachers and others. But Tyler's big break came during a babysitting job for one of the Vice Presidents at Merrill Lynch, Malcolm Taaffe. Mr. Taaffe was so impressed with Tyler that he offered the youth an internship that turned into a full-time job only two weeks later! Tyler left this job to start CoolTronics at the age of fifteen, and built a computer repair shop into an outlet that sells, delivers and sets up PCs for its customers. In charge of a business that does millions in sales each year, Tyler was named one of the Top 25 entrepreneurs under the age of twenty-five by Businessweek.

Lesson: Don't be afraid to extend yourself and try out different things. One of them just might put you in the right place at the right time, making all of your dreams come true.

MICHAEL DUNLOP OF INCOMEDIARY

A high school dropout who struggled with dyslexia, Michael has earned the respect of the business world with his website Income-Diary. Despite numerous teachers telling him he was sure to fail, his sound business advice now earns him a pretty penny each year and allows him to work only "one to four hours" a day. Michael also founded the site Retireat21.com, which shows that despite all of his success, he remains focused on living the good life forever.

Lesson: You have a better sense of your abilities than anyone else so don't listen to those who try to keep you down.

JOHN MAGENNIS AND WEB DESIGN

John, like a lot of kids, taught himself web design at a young age. But he was also an excellent teacher and an unbelievably quick learner. In no time at all, he went from charging $15 per site to $30,000, and was designing websites for Fortune 500 companies. That kind of money adds up quickly, and John earned his first million by the age of sixteen. John then moved on to produce reality television shows, such as The Bachelor and Celebrity Apprentice!

Lesson: Don't be afraid to start small. If you've got the ability, people and their money will find you.

KIOWA KAVOVIT OF BOO BOO GOO

Kiowa is the youngest entrepreneur to appear on Shark Tank to date. She was only six when she had the idea for Boo Boo Goo, a paint-on bandage for kids. Even more incredible, she was so charming and articulate that she came away from the show with a $100,000 investment! Kiowa has rewarded the faith shown in her by becoming a millionaire in 2014.

Lesson: A great idea is important, but if you can get the message across to others there's no limit to what you can do.

DIANE KENG OF MYWEBOO

Diane's incredible drive was ignited by a high school that encouraged entrepreneurship and the dissatisfaction of her $15-a-week allowance. Diane founded a T-shirt company and a business that helps companies market to teenagers, but MyWeboo, a service that helps teens manage their online reputation, is what she's best known for.

Lesson: You don't have to accept what the world offers you. If you're unhappy with it, try to take matters into your own hands.

MADISON ROBINSON OF FISH FLOPS

Madison started Fish Flops at fifteen, selling flip-flops with designs geared toward teenagers. The early success of these encouraged her to expand her product lines and build a complimentary app. Madison's line was such a big hit that she had $1 million in sales before she could even drive! She's now pushed her wares onto the shelves at national giants like Nordstrom and Macy's.

Lessons: Pay attention to what people in a certain age group are wearing. If you can figure out how they want to look, you can position yourself for a major score.

DOMINIC MCVEY AND SCOOTERS

Having stumbled upon Viza, a scooter company, while trying to search for Visa, Dominic quickly realized that he'd struck gold. By virtue of his keen business eye, he recognized that the strength of the British pound made for a considerable price discrepancy between scooters in the UK and the US. He began importing scooters and selling them around London at the age of thirteen. A millionaire by fifteen, Dominic is now worth around $10 million!

Lesson: Be on the lookout for every advantage. A million-dollar opportunity may be lying in plain sight.

TEN GREAT WAYS TO . . .

WHAT YOU'LL LEARN:

- Where to Find Stock Market Advice
- Websites to Find More About Starting a Business

BUSINESS IDEAS COVERED:

☑ Make money from home

☑ Jobs available in your neighborhood

☑ Ways to monetize your creativity

☑ Sporty/athletic ways to make money

TEN GREAT WAYS TO
MAKE MONEY FROM HOME

Stuck watching your younger siblings? Confined to your house because your parents want you to focus on your studies? Feel more comfortable in your home than anywhere else? Don't worry, you can still cash in!

1. Watch YouTube

A company named InboxDollars (inboxdollars.com) will pay you to watch videos on YouTube. They may not be as riveting as the clips you share with your friends, but there are worse ways to scrape some cash together.

2. Fill out surveys

But before you do, please proceed with caution. There is no shortage of sketchy websites who promise big rewards for filling out surveys and fail to deliver. SwagBucks and Ipsos i-Say (Ipsos conducts a lot of the presidential election polls) are two legitimate surveys that will compensate you for your opinions.

3. Fixing search engines

Ever type something into Google and been confused by what came up? You may have discovered an error in Google's famous search algorithm. Yes, even Google makes mistakes. You can get paid to fix them as a "search engine evaluator"! If you're interested in doing this check out Leapforce or Lionbridge. These are two of the leading companies in search engine evaluation.

4. Offer to organize mom or dad's paperwork

Take a look at your parents' desk. Odds are, it's a bit of mess. Their lives are so busy, there's not enough time to keep everything in order. That's where you come in! Offer to file papers for them.

You'll likely save them from something they've been dreading.

5. Test websites

Feel like you've got an eye for what it takes to make a good website? A company named UserTesting will pay you to visit websites and apps and evaluate them with an assigned set of tasks. You will then be asked to voice your opinion about the whole experience.

6. Amazon Mechanical Turk

This is a marketplace that allows businesses access to individuals who have mastered the tasks their computers still struggle computing. The tasks are easy and you can complete them at your convenience, so take a look!

7. Write for Listverse

Find it difficult to resist listicles? You're not alone. They've taken over the Internet, and Listverse will pay you $100 for an original, interesting list consisting of 10 items.

8. Sell your photos

Are people always looking at your photos or telling you that you've got a good eye? A new app named Foap allows you to sell your personal photos for cash! All you have to do is upload a photo and set the price for other people to license it. You'll get paid each time someone does.

9. Transcribe

Check Craigslist for opportunities to transcribe everything from audio recordings to medical records. This work may be pretty tedious, but it should pay well and will do wonders for your vocabulary and typing skills.

10. Become an expert

Love to learn about new things? Now you can turn that drive into cold, hard cash! Visit the website ChaCha.com, which pays up to $9.00 an hour for researching the answers to their obscure questions.

TEN GREAT JOBS AVAILABLE RIGHT IN YOUR NEIGHBORHOOD

If you know what to look for, your own neighborhood is loaded with opportunities to make money!

1. Spreading bark mulch

You've seen it piled in people's driveways but you may not have realized that each one is a golden opportunity to make money. If you see one of your neighbors getting mulch delivered, offer to spread it for them. Chances are they were reserving precious weekend time for it and will be thrilled to get it off their plate.

2. Clearing the snow off people's cars

This will require you to get up early, but if you can guarantee your customer's cars will be cleared off by the time they have to go to work, you will be all set. It's a pretty good gig: you make some money and you make someone else's day. And afterward, you can head back to bed!

3. Gardening & planting

Live in an area where the homeowners are into gardening? Love to watch things grow? Love fresh vegetables or flowers? Offer to help water and weed your neighbors' gardens. You'll learn more about what different types of plants prefer and can spend your days in the sunshine.

4. Babysitting

If there are a lot of young children in your neighborhood, babysitting is a great way to make money. It's also something you can do all the way through college. In order to gain people's full confidence, sign up for a babysitting course. They are usually offered through local hospitals and medical clinics. The course will provide CPR training and other valuable information, such as how to deal with emergencies and crises that may arise while you're watching a small child.

5. Raking

Whether it is leaves in the fall or dead grass in the spring, there's always plenty of raking to do and not much interest in doing it. Take advantage of people's reluctance and position yourself as the neighborhood's designated raker. You'll have no shortage of work!

6. Washing/detailing cars

People want their cars to look sharp but typically don't have the time to do this themselves. Invest in some cleaning supplies and make the neighborhood's autos shine, inside and out! If you enjoy cars, this is a great way to get into the business side of that world.

7. Cleaning out/organizing people's garages and sheds

You may have noticed a few garages that resemble the pile of clothes threatening to escape your closet. As busy as everyone is, things pile up pretty quickly and get to a point of utter chaos. Step in and give them their garage space back. They'll be beyond grateful.

8. Tarring driveways

If you live in a place with harsh winters, you can bet that there are plenty of cracked driveways. Ice works its way into these cracks and can make a big mess if it is ignored for too long. You can keep this from happening with a little bit of sweat and a lot of tar. It'll be sticky and hot but you can make good money with very little initial investment.

9. Painting

People have all kinds of stuff that needs to be painted: doors, fences, sheds, and houses. These are also items that are constantly in need of being repainted. If you're able to make things look nice and neat, you'll never lack for work.

10. Pet-sitting/dog walker

A lot of the time, people are reluctant to go away because of their pets. You can ease the owners' minds and provide their pet with some companionship when it would otherwise be alone, or in a kennel. On top of that, you'll make money for pretty easy work. Everybody wins!

TEN GREAT WAYS TO MONETIZE YOUR CREATIVITY

Tired of hearing people say artists don't make any money? Try your hand at a few of these and show them just how misguided that belief is.

1. Dress up inexpensive items

Use your good taste to take less expensive things and create something of greater value. One example is a mason jar, some white paint and twine. On their own they're nothing special, but combined in the right way they become something appealing and charming such as a decorative vase or toothbrush cup!

2. Fiverr

Fiverr is a marketplace where people can list the services they provide for as little as $5. From editing photos to drawings to recording sound, there's a market for almost every skill!

3. Print T-shirts

If you have graphic design talent, T-shirts can be a great way to display your skills. Create a few designs and print them on a shirt for yourself. If the response is enthusiastic, you know you've found a potential moneymaker. Print some more up and see if you can sell them.

4. Make jewelry

You can sell your handmade designs on Etsy or even to your classmates! Since you won't have to pay rent on a storefront or for salespeople, you'll be able to offer it at a lower price than a store and still ensure yourself a profit.

5. Build toys

Do you remember looking at your toys and wishing they were more appealing or had a couple more functions? Take matters into your own hands and design toys that will dazzle those younger than you.

6. Key chains, lanyards, and wallets

These are three items almost everyone uses. Depending on the material you choose, the cost for the materials should be pretty low compared to what you can sell them for. Use an engraver to personalize key chains or buy a branding iron to dress up what would typically be just a boring old brown leather wallet.

7. Knitting

More and more people today are looking to distinguish themselves with some striking, funky accessory. If you can knit, get to work on creating some wild scarves or socks that can help them stand out!

8. Take painting and drawing commissions

Gifted at drawing or painting? Your talent can provide others with a unique memento that commemorates the things they love. Offer up your talents! It's a great way to get to practice and ultimately pay for supplies/art classes.

9. Become a DJ

If you're obsessed with music, DJing is a great way for you to capitalize on your terrific ear. If someone in your school is throwing a party, offer to provide the music for a fee. If they're on the fence, ask them what kind of music they envision playing and toss together a mix that shows off your skills.

10. Decorate cakes

Whether someone is having a wedding, a graduation party, or celebrating a birthday, they are looking for cakes that are increasingly elaborate. Do your part to fill the demand. With your exacting nature, attention to detail and technical prowess you're sure to go far in this profession.

TEN GREAT WAYS TO FIND STOCK MARKET ADVICE

Are you a stock market junkie? These outlets won't just provide a fix they'll also give you great advice.

1. Bloomberg TV and CNBC

These channels are two pillars of the financial press. Tune in and see which individuals you are drawn to. Take notes on the picks they recommend and track their performance. When you find someone who is helping you view the market accurately and in an enjoyable way, make time to see what they have to say.

2. The Motley Fool

You have to pay for advice from these guys, but since they've had a number of great picks through the years (including Netflix and Tesla) it's worth it!

3. Reddit stock market thread

Reddit is an online version of the corkboard at your café. Users can constantly post links and content that intrigues them. At times, the thread can get bogged down by trolls and spammers but if you know who to pay attention to, there's some really sound and investing advice in here.

4. Yahoo! Finance message boards

Due to the tremendous amount of activity on these boards, they're a great way to gain perspective and information on the stocks you have a hunch about!

5. Seeking Alpha (seekingalpha.com)

This website provides news on the market and advice on stocks, but it is their informative overviews of companies that make it a must to bookmark on your browser.

6. Twitter

If you follow knowledgeable traders who frequently post, you can find some excellent advice on Twitter. Follow those traders with more than a 1,000 followers and watch the stocks that they tweet. You're not only looking for how the stock performs, but at what point the trader got in or out.

7. 24/7 Wall St. (247Wallst.com)

This is a great site for financial news and opinions. They publish over 30 articles a day and refrain from investing in the companies they write about so you can trust them to be objective.

8. Minyanville (minyanville.com)

This site is a go-to for cutting edge news and financial guidance. It employs a knowledgeable staff that includes traders and money managers who team up to provide a ton of specialized content and great insight.

9. StreetInsider.com

Positioning itself as the ultimate Wall Street insider, this site features an overwhelming amount of resources and is a great place to find information on any new investment arena you are considering.

10. Investment Contrarians (investmentcontrarians.com)

This blog provides outstanding advice and insight into the market. As they are one of the few outlets who correctly predicted the housing crisis, you can trust that their thinking, while outside the box, is sound. In addition to their blog, they also offer a newsletter.

TEN GREAT SPORTY/ATHLETIC WAYS TO MAKE MONEY

If you're an athlete, you don't need to make it to the big leagues to earn money. Check out the list below to find interesting ways to turn your athletic ability into profit!

1. Become a coach/trainer

If you possess extraordinary athletic ability, many people will be to be interested in finding out how you've mastered your level of skill. Consider hiring yourself out to help others get that higher level. It'll be fun and will help you think about your own expertise in a different way.

2. Offer to teach swimming lessons to the kids in your neighborhood

Want to spend all day in your pool? If you're a very strong swimmer, you may be able to convince parents to let you teach their children this valuable skill.

3. Referee/Umpire

Local leagues are always on the lookout for officials. It's a great way to make extra money and gain a unique perspective of your favorite game.

4. Lifeguard

Working on your tan and saving people's lives sounds like a pretty good opportunity, doesn't it? You will need to take a weekend-long course to get certified and complete CPR training, but you'll have a job that you can continue all the way through college!

5. Caddy

Your golf course may have a caddy program, but if not, don't let that stop you! Offer your services to the top players at the course. You'll not only make good money, you'll learn even more by watching these highly talented golfers.

6. Build skateboard ramps

If you're into skateboarding, you know how difficult it is to find a place where you can practice without being hassled. Ensure that you and your friends always have somewhere to go by building your own ramps and halfpipes! If your workmanship is up to snuff, you'll be able to sell these items for a pretty penny.

7. Start a YouTube series where you teach others how to acquire your skills

Have someone film you performing the drills that have helped you to become an accomplished athlete. If you garner a large enough audience, you'll be able to make money while also positioning yourself for a career in coaching.

8. Bike messenger

If you can't find enough time to ride your bike, you may want to turn that passion into a paid gig. You'll build up your skills and stamina racing all over town, and you'll meet a bunch of new people.

9. Start a league

In most towns, the baseball leagues are finished before school gets out. Be proactive and start a summer league. There's no better time to play than during those warm summer months. You'll have a blast and will learn numerous valuable lessons in the process of organizing it. It doesn't have to be baseball. Volleyball, 3-on-3 basketball, lacrosse, or Ultimate Frisbee are other great options.

10. Work at a sports camp

The summer is filled with all kinds of camps devoted to various sports. If you've attended any of them in the past and enjoyed it, see about getting brought on as a counselor or staff member. You'll be able to pick your co-workers brains all day long and you're getting paid.

TEN GREAT WEBSITES TO LEARN ABOUT STARTING A BUSINESS

Thinking about starting a business but unsure of where to start? A review of these websites will point you in the right direction!

1. Entrepreneur.com

Full of marketing tips, events and analysis, this site provides guidance on which smartphone is best suited to your needs to how to improve your marketing strategies to specific demographics.

2. Businessknowhow.com

A great site for small business owners and individuals who are self-employed. The site produces a steady stream of articles that will give you ideas on how to retain employees, how to motivate yourself when you're having trouble starting your company, and how to improve your networking ability.

3. Score.org

They "offer the nation's largest network of free, expert business mentors," and also provide guidance and resources to help you get started. If you're struggling with any aspect of your business, chances are this site will be able to suggest a solution.

4. Bplans.com

Have a big idea but unsure of how you can make it attractive to potential investors? This site offers you templates for everything from business plans to pitch presentations.

5. Inc.com

This site is the go-to for the latest happenings in the entrepreneurial world. Inc. also offers great analysis, identification of trends, and in-depth features on your business heroes.

6. Startuplawyer.com

Intimidated by all the legal details that go into starting your own business? Don't worry, it's a common feeling. And, lucky for you, Startup Lawyer has you covered, providing great information on the legal issues that come up during a startup's ascendance.

7. allBusiness.com

When these folks say all, they mean all. Offering tips on everything from starting a business to office etiquette, they're ready to resolve any nagging doubts or questions you may have.

8. forEntrepreneurs.com

This blog is the brainchild of David Skok, a five-time entrepreneur, who kindly shares the lessons learned during his time at the venture capital firm, Matrix Partners. Featuring helpful techniques, charts and models, the content is data-centric but accessible.

9. Brazen.com

Don't let the arrogance suggested by the name fool you. This site scores major points for its no-nonsense, easy to understand business-related content. Full of insightful blogs, informative eBooks and educational webinars, they can school you in whatever medium you prefer.

10. Noobpreneur.com

This online magazine provides award-winning content that is geared toward the small business owner and those who are considering becoming one. As a site that believes in the power offered by a variety of perspectives, they also accept submissions for potential publication!

TEN GREAT MOVIES FEATURING RICH KIDS

Looking to relax and be inspired along the way? Unwind with these movies.

1. Richie Rich

Macaulay Culkin is the world's richest kid and has everything you could ever want and more. But, after encountering a group of neighborhood kids playing sandlot baseball, he finds that life is about far more than our material possessions.

2. Wild Child

Emma Roberts plays California rich girl Poppy Moore, who is such a troublemaker that she gets sent to a boarding school in England to be disciplined. Instead of continuing her rebellious ways, Poppy discovers abilities and strengths she never knew she had, and returns to California a changed person.

3. Prince Caspian

Part of the excellent Chronicles of Narnia film series, this installment follows the Pevensie children as they aid Prince Caspian in his quest to regain the throne that is rightfully his.

4. Uptown Girls

Dakota Fanning plays Ray, who is about as serious as an eight-year-old can be. However, when her new nanny, Molly takes over and teaches Ray how to enjoy life, this one-time wallflower begins to flourish.

5. Annie (1999)

An eleven-year-old orphan, Annie manages to escape the evil clutches of Miss Hannigan thanks to Daddy Warbucks, a billionaire who decides to adopt her. Unsure of each other at first, Daddy Warbucks and Annie soon partner to find Annie's real parents and avoid the evil designs of Miss Hannigan.

6. Hannah Montana: The Movie

As Miley Stewart's alter ego, Hannah Montana begins to encroach on her personal life and takes a trip back home to revisit her roots and put things into perspective.

7. Blank Check

A comedy that details the adventures of twelve-year-old Preston

Waters. After a bank robber runs over Preston's bicycle and hands him a blank check to buy a new one, Preston fills it out for $1 million and then embarks on an epic shopping- spree. All the while the bank robber and his associates are trying to catch up with him.

8. Clueless

In this hilarious depiction of wealthy youths in Beverly Hills, Alicia Silverstone is the queen of her school's social hierarchy. But when she gets a wakeup call from her stepbrother Josh (Paul Rudd), her whole perspective on life changes.

9. The Princess Diaries

Anne Hathaway gets to live out every kid's dream when she is transported out of her dreary life in San Francisco to become a princess and heir to the throne of Genovia.

10. Troop Beverly Hills

This is a hilarious adventure that follows a Girl Scout troop as they navigate the "wilds of Beverly Hills" and attempt to become recognized by the regional council.

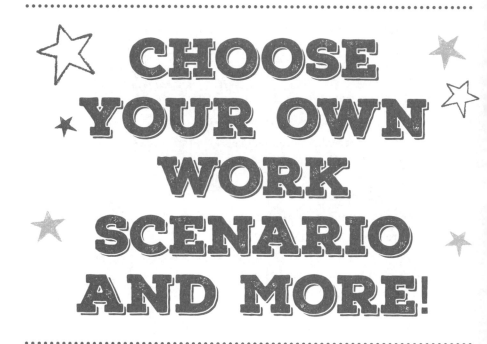

CHOOSE YOUR OWN WORK SCENARIO AND MORE!

WHAT YOU'LL LEARN:

- How to Work with Friends
- Communicating with Employees
- The stock market ups and downs
- Networking
- Finding a Mentor

Test your strengths as a business owner with the flowing work scenarios. Good luck!

GAME 1: HIRING EMPLOYEES

A year ago you started a lawn-care business. It did so well that heading into this summer you not only have all your clients from last year, but an additional twenty who signed up because of all the positive buzz. In order to take on these new customers and still provide the level of work that brought them to you, you know you're going to have to hire a helper. You put the word out and find two people who are interested in the job: your good friend, Ryan, and Tyler, who is intelligent, hard working and nice, but you aren't that close.

You're certain that you and Ryan will have such a blast, so you decide to hire him. After celebrating and talking about all the fun you're going to have together, you tell him that he'll be making $9.00/hour, a detail that got lost in all the excitement. You've run the numbers and determined that this is the most you can afford to pay someone while still taking in some commission. Unfortunately, Ryan laughs when you tell him this and says he won't work for anything less than $11.00/hour. What do you do?

Option 1
* Agree to give Ryan the rate he's asking for. If you choose this option, proceed to page 105.

Option 2
* Tell him you'll think about it with the intention of compromising. If you prefer this path, proceed to page 106.

Option 3
* Stick to your guns and tell him that's the best you can do, knowing that if he refuses to accept it, you can always hire Tyler. If this is your choice, proceed to page 107.

GIVE RYAN THE RATE HE REQUESTED

You didn't want to upset your friend, so you agreed to his salary demands. Now that you've started working together, you find yourself constantly feeling as though Ryan isn't working as hard as you had hoped. You're having plenty of fun, but you consistently have to help him with the tasks you've assigned and re-do those he does complete to make sure they meet the level your customers have come to expect from you.

When you agreed to the higher rate, you figured that, since you weren't going to make as much with Ryan on-board, you would at least finish the jobs quicker and not have to put in as many hours as you did last summer. Except you're two weeks in and not only are you making less than you'd like, the jobs are taking just as long. And because of all the new accounts, you're putting in way more hours than you did. What do you do?

* Say nothing and just deal with your frustrations. If you choose this, proceed to the below paragraph.

* Tell Ryan that since you agreed to pay him the higher rate, you need a better effort from him. If you choose this option, proceed to page 110.

THOSE WHO CHOSE TO SAY NOTHING

You're now in mid-July. Ryan is starting to get the hang of it, but his effort is still not up to par. You find that you have to spend a lot of time working on the opposite side of the property from Ryan, otherwise you'll get angry when watching him work and say something unkind out of frustration.

As the days grow hotter and the long hours pile up, you find yourself debating whether you even want to do this next summer, despite all your efforts to build up the company and your customer base.

PROCEED TO PAGE 112

THOSE WHO CHOSE TO TELL RYAN THAT HE NEEDS TO STEP IT UP

Upon confronting Ryan, he acted surprised and said: "I thought we were friends." Almost immediately a switch flipped inside of you and all the frustration that had been building up came out. An argument was had before you both walked away. You cooled down, talked later that day and patched things up. But in the days that followed there was no difference in the quality of his effort, way fewer laughs than when you started and much more silence.

Money and exhaustion aren't even your main concerns any longer. Now you spend your days trying to think of a way that you can salvage both your friendship with Ryan and your business. No matter what you come up with it, it seems like one or the other will be affected.

PROCEED TO PAGE 112

FOR THOSE WHO CHOSE TO THINK ABOUT IT

After taking a couple of days to weigh the pros and cons of a number of options, you decide to offer Ryan a choice. He can either accept $10.00/hour or he can start at $9.00/hour and you will evaluate his work after two weeks. Then, if he is doing the work that is deserving of more money, you have no problem giving it to him.

To your delight, he takes the second option! With the added motivation of impressing you and earning a raise, he performs way beyond your expectations.

You keep your word and give him the higher rate that he asked for. You can now send him to do a job by himself and know that he'll do it right so you are working less, still making good money, and continuing to build the business, all with the help of one of your good friends.

PROCEED TO PAGE 112

FOR THOSE WHO STUCK TO THEIR GUNS

Knowing that you had a backup plan with Tyler, you told Ryan that $9.00/hour was your final offer. He said he wasn't going to work that rate for an entire summer and refused to take the job.

You did hire Tyler, who gladly accepted the $9.00/hour. He's picked things up quickly and does excellent work. Now you don't have to do quite as much as you did last summer and are making good money.

But as great as things are from a business perspective, your social life has taken a hit. When Ryan walked and you had to hire Tyler, you were hoping to become better friends as you spent time more together. Sadly, there is not much talking between the two of you during work and you can't help but wish Ryan were there beside you.

Meanwhile, you've seen Ryan a couple of times but things have been tenser than you would like. You still joke around and play video games, but he freezes up any time you mention work. You constantly wonder if you should have gone another route when he asked for the higher rate.

PROCEED TO PAGE 112

GAME 1 LESSONS

As you've just seen, mixing business and friendship can be extremely challenging. Your relationship has to be strong and completely honest if it's going to be able to withstand the pressures of working together.

It's not solely about the money issue or about being able to tell your friend they've done something wrong. You may be friends, but under the stress of a work environment, it's easy for people to take things personally and get bent out of shape, so be sure you're choosing your working partner wisely.

You may have been better off going with Tyler right off the bat (Kudos to those who thought this as they were reading!) and telling Ryan that you like him too much to jeopardize your friendship over something silly like lawn care. If he still seems upset, offer him an opportunity to help out on Tyler's day's off.

But, since this game was not concerned with the hiring of Ryan but rather with his salary request, let's take a closer look at each option and the lessons available in each.

OPTION 1

If you decide to immediately give Ryan the money he is asking for, you have just decided to value your enjoyment at work over the money you're making. And that's absolutely fine! There's a lot to be said for making your work environment as fun as you can and prioritizing this over money. But it's important to realize that this decision, like every decision, carries a price.

If you're interested in having a good time while you're working, chances are you'll have to give up some of your earning power. Giving Ryan the money he asks for before laying down the expectations of the job, guarantees that you'll be disappointed and frustrated. It will also end up putting you in a position where you're giving up both money and enjoyment. So it's important to see the outcomes of your decisions right from the very start.

OPTION 2

This choice creates two valuable things for any business owner: an option and a way to provide motivation. By telling Ryan that his compensation was tied to his performance, you gave yourself a way out if things do not go well, made him eager to prove himself, and also indicated the level of effort and quality that is expected. And you were able to accomplish all that just by being considerate and fair, without having to become stern and boss your friend around.

This is a good strategy to utilize with any new employee who is hesitant to accept your initial salary offer. Let them know that this is your rate during the initial, "probationary" period, and tell them that if things work out and they exceed expectations, you are absolutely open to discussing a higher pay rate. This kind of fairness and subtle setting of expectations will go a long way, making you someone people will want to work for instead of someone they have to work for.

OPTION 3

This may have been the best decision for your bottom line, but this kind of stubbornness rarely bodes well for the long-term health of a business. To run a successful business you need flexibility, and you can only get this by keeping your options open and prioritizing your relationships with people.

Because you had Tyler waiting in the wings, you knew you could afford to stand firm with Ryan and still get what you want: an employee making $9.00/hour. But this makes Ryan feel as though you haven't heard him at all, and if something should happen with Tyler (he hurts his leg while climbing a tree, or he decides the work is too boring and quits), you're going to be in a tough spot. Ryan isn't going to be itching to come help you out.

It went as smoothly as it could this time, but eventually this kind of inflexibility is going to catch up with you and leave you in a precarious position. So, when someone makes a request, don't immediately dismiss it and remain focused on what you want. Instead, do your best to find a middle ground, a solution that benefits both parties and not just you.

GAME 2: STOCKS

You just spent the summer lifeguarding. After covering your expenses and socking some money away in a savings account, you have $1,500 to invest. You're interested in trying out the stock market and you've been following a number of websites and reputable financial blogs. After much research, you've narrowed your search down to two stocks. The first is a biotech startup with a hot new hearing device set to come on the market. Their shares are only $5.00 a piece. The second is an established delivery service that people are predicting a good-sized jump in due to an expected drop in oil prices. This company's shares, which are notoriously steady, are trading at $10.00. Do you:

Option 1
* Invest all $1,500 in the hot new company. If you choose this please proceed to page 111.

Option 2
* Invest all $1,500 in the delivery service. If you choose this pleas proceed to page 111.

Option 3

* Invest $1,000 in the hot new company and $500 in the delivery service. If you choose this please proceed to page 112.

Option 4

* Invest $1,000 in the delivery service and $500 in the hot new company. If you choose this please proceed to page 113.

INVEST ALL IN THE BIOTECH COMPANY

One week after you make your investment, the stock zooms up to $12.00 a share. Since the blog that introduced you to the stock predicts that it will go even higher, you resist the urge to sell and cash out your $2,100 profit.

Two weeks later, the stock has not exploded as predicted but instead sits at $13.50 a share, leaving you feeling pretty good about staying with it. You spend most of your days dreaming about what you're going to spend your money on when the stock takes its next leap.

Then, during the first week of November, the FDA announces that they will not approve the new device and the stock plunges all the way down to $3.00, erasing all of your profits and $600 of your initial investment.

PROCEED TO PAGE 117

INVEST ALL IN THE DELIVERY SERVICE

The predicted drop in oil never came and the stock price has drifted between $9.50 and $11.25 for months. During the first week of November, the stock sits at $11.00.

While the $150 in profit is nice (a 10% return, far better than you would be able to get from any savings account or CD), you were hoping for something a little more exciting, for a taste of that exhilaration you've heard the stock market provides.

You decide to sell off half your shares to put $400 in your savings account and use the rest to purchase 200 shares of a new startup that has people buzzing.

PROCEED TO PAGE 117

$1,000 ON THE STARTUP AND $500 ON THE DELIVERY SERVICE

One week after you make your investment, the biotech stock zooms up to $12.00 a share. Since the blog that introduced you to the stock predicts that it will go even higher, you resist the urge to sell and cash out your $1,400 profit.

Two weeks later, the stock has not exploded as predicted but still sits at $13.50 a share, leaving you feeling pretty good about staying with it.

Then, during the first week of November, the FDA announces that they will not approve the new device and the stock plunges all the way down to $3.00, erasing all of your profits and $400 of your initial investment.

But all is not lost!

The predicted drop in oil never came and the delivery company's stock has drifted between $9.50 and $11.25 for months. During the same first week of November, the stock sits at $11.00 and while the $50 in profit isn't going to make you rich, a 10% return is far better than you would have been able to get from any savings account or CD. And, compared to the roller coaster ride your other stock took, this kind of reliable return doesn't seem so bad.

PROCEED TO PAGE 117

$1,000 IN THE DELIVERY SERVICE AND $500 IN THE BIOTECH STARTUP

One week after you make your investment, the biotech company's stock zooms up to $12.00 a share. Since the blog that introduced you to the stock predicts that it will go even higher, you resist the urge to sell and cash out your $700 profit.

Two weeks later, the stock has not exploded as predicted but still sits at $13.50 a share, leaving you feeling pretty good about staying with it.

Then, during the first week of November, the FDA announces that the device failed in the last round of testing and they will not approve it. The stock plunges all the way down to $3.00, erasing all of your profits and $200 of your initial investment.

But all is not lost!

The predicted drop in oil never came and the delivery company's stock has drifted between $9.50 and $11.25 for months. During the same first week of November, the stock sits at $11.00 and while the $100 in profit isn't going to make you rich, a 10% return is far better than you would have been able to get from any savings account or CD. And, compared to the roller coaster ride your other stock took, this kind of reliable return doesn't seem so bad.

PROCEED TO the Game 2 Lessons below.

GAME 2 LESSONS

A few valuable examples are set-up right from the start in this game. It is common for a lesser-known stock to garner buzz based on its new offering. It is also common for this buzz to allow the stock to take off before any product is produced. This is not to say that the buzz is never accurate, or that there are no small, unknown companies ready to take the world by storm (think about those jumping on Apple or Amazon stock in its early days). But, more often than not, the hype and thrill of the roller coaster ride are all you're going to end up with from these investments.

They will pay off big if you get them right, but you're going to have to sift through a lot of losers. Your stomach will also constantly be in knots by all these turbulent rides. If you're the type who lives for the thrill of a big score consider a route like Option 4. In order to make risky, high-reward investments, without blowing through all your money, you're going to need to hedge your bets with a bunch of solid, reliable plays that will keep the money trickling in. This will keep your losses small and also provide money for your long shots.

What's really interesting about this scenario is that Option 2: the boring, steady stock making a big leap, is actually an ideal investment opportunity. You should be very excited when you see this in the stock market.

The predicted drop in oil prices gives you is known as a freeroll. The stock's long-term, steady performance provides you with almost no chance of losing your money. There's also a very good chance you're going to make a lot if the predicted drop is large. Be on the lookout for opportunities like this, where there is very little risk and tons of reward. Once you do spot one, don't be afraid to put all your eggs in the basket.

This game is attempting to illustrate why you don't want the excitement of playing the stock market to come from volatile and unpredictable stocks. Instead, you want to be excited by the hunt and discovery of opportunities, just like the delivery service and the drop in oil prices presented. Once you get as excited about recognizing one of these opportunities as you do about getting in on the latest hot new stock, you'll know you're on the right track.

FINANCE TEMPLATES AND CHARTS TO GET YOU STARTED!

KEEP TRACK OF YOUR BUSINESS' FINANCES!

This way you can keep an eye on your company's expenses and income, without losing money or going into "the red"!

Date	Product or Service	Price (+)	Expense (−)	Total (=)
1/1/16	Lawn mowing at 72 Oak St	$50	$5 gas for mower	$45
1/15/16	Landscaping at 14 Oriole St	$120	$15 for gas	$105
1/19/16	Shoveling snow at 210 Elm	$20	None	$20
1/21/16	Pulling weeds at 51 Lewis	$30	None	$30
	TOTAL	$220	$20	$200

Date	Product or Service	Price (+)	Expense (−)	Total (=)

A PARENT-APPROVED CHORE CHART!

You can help out around the house with chores and build up your savings! Work out the rates and frequency with your parents, or make separate charts for indoor and outdoor chores.

Chore	Frequency	Days	Rate (weekly)
Mow the lawn	Once a week	Sunday	$20
Take out the trash	Twice a week	Tue & Fri	$10
Walk the dog	Daily	Daily	$50
Wash the dishes	Four times a week	Mon–Thu	$20
		TOTAL	$100

Chore	Frequency	Days	Rate (weekly)

KEEP TRACK OF YOUR PIGGY BANK!

Jot down how much you earned this month, and how you spent it. The more you save, the more you'll have for bigger and better purchases!

Date	Description	Spent	Earned	Total
2/1/16	Shoveling snow	$0	$20	+$20
2/5/16	Babysitting	$0	$50	+$50
			Total	+$70
2/10/16	Video Game	$30	$0	−$30
			Total	+$40

Date	Description	Spent	Earned	Total

INDEX

ABOUT APPLESAUCE PRESS

What kid doesn't love Applesauce!
Good ideas ripen with time. From seed to harvest, Applesauce Press crafts books with beautiful designs, creative formats, and kid-friendly information on a variety of topics. Like our parent company, Cider Mill Press Book Publishers, our press bears fruit twice a year, publishing a new crop of titles each spring and fall.

"Where Good Books Are Ready for Press"

Visit us on the web at
www.cidermillpress.com

or write to us at
PO Box 454
12 Spring Street
Kennebunkport, ME 04046